I0454675

Editor-in-Chief and Founder:
  Lyndon H. LaRouche, Jr.
Editorial Board: *Lyndon H. LaRouche, Jr. , Helga Zepp-LaRouche, Robert Ingraham, Tony Papert, Gerald Rose, Dennis Small, Jeffrey Steinberg, William Wertz*
Co-Editors: *Robert Ingraham, Tony Papert*
Managing Editor: *Nancy Spannaus*
Technology: *Marsha Freeman*
Books: *Katherine Notley*
Ebooks: *Richard Burden*
Graphics: *Alan Yue*
Photos: *Stuart Lewis*
Circulation Manager: *Stanley Ezrol*

INTELLIGENCE DIRECTORS
Counterintelligence: *Jeffrey Steinberg, Michele Steinberg*
Economics: *John Hoefle, Marcia Merry Baker, Paul Gallagher*
History: *Anton Chaitkin*
Ibero-America: *Dennis Small*
Russia and Eastern Europe: *Rachel Douglas*
United States: *Debra Freeman*

INTERNATIONAL BUREAUS
Bogotá: *Miriam Redondo*
Berlin: *Rainer Apel*
Copenhagen: *Tom Gillesberg*
Houston: *Harley Schlanger*
Lima: *Sara Madueño*
Melbourne: *Robert Barwick*
Mexico City: *Gerardo Castilleja Chávez*
New Delhi: *Ramtanu Maitra*
Paris: *Christine Bierre*
Stockholm: *Ulf Sandmark*
United Nations, N.Y.C.: *Leni Rubinstein*
Washington, D.C.: *William Jones*
Wiesbaden: *Göran Haglund*

ON THE WEB
e-mail: eirns@larouchepub.com
www.larouchepub.com
www.executiveintelligencereview.com
www.larouchepub.com/eiw
Webmaster: *John Sigerson*
Assistant Webmaster: *George Hollis*
Editor, Arabic-language edition: *Hussein Askary*

EIR (ISSN 0273-6314) *is published weekly (50 issues), by EIR News Service, Inc., P.O. Box 17390, Washington, D.C. 20041-0390. (703) 777-9451 ext. 415*

European Headquarters: E.I.R. GmbH, Postfach Bahnstrasse 9a, D-65205, Wiesbaden, Germany
Tel: 49-611-73650
Homepage: http://www.eirna.com
e-mail: eirna@eirna.com
Director: Georg Neudecker

Montreal, Canada: 514-461-1557

Denmark: EIR - Danmark, Sankt Knuds Vej 11, basement left, DK-1903 Frederiksberg, Denmark. Tel.: +45 35 43 60 40, Fax: +45 35 43 87 57. e-mail: eirdk@hotmail.com.

Mexico City: EIR, Sor Juana Inés de la Cruz 242-2 Col. Agricultura C.P. 11360 Delegación M. Hidalgo, México D.F. Tel. (5525) 5318-2301 eirmexico@gmail.com

Canada Post Publication Sales Agreement #40683579

Postmaster: Send all address changes to *EIR*, P.O. Box 17390, Washington, D.C. 20041-0390.

The Great Opportunity Of September

EDITORIAL

OBAMA IS A FAILURE

The World Needs a New Financial Architecture Now!

Aug. 26—Obama must be ousted, regardless of how much time is left, if there is to be any functioning New Presidency in the United States during the period ahead. His Presidency has been a failure, one which is wreaking havoc, death, and chaos on the United States and the world through illegal wars, bailouts, drone attacks, the destruction of healthcare, drug-related deaths, unemployment, and Obama's personal psychotic pathology. As the nations of Eurasia, under the leadership of President Putin, construct a new strategic and economic system, Obama must be condemned for what he is: an abject failure and a servant of the dying British Monarchy.

It is the ongoing collaboration between the leadership of Russia and China on a new economic system and urgent structural changes to the global financial system, which is of the utmost importance. This is the critical flank to avoid nuclear world war and financial chaos—the results of Obama's failed Presidency—and this is the leading topic of discussion among world leaders during the many international summits over the months of September and October.

President Xi Jinping of China intends to put the critical issue of a new world economic and financial system on the agenda of the upcoming G-20 Summit in Hangzhou, China. The offi-cial China media, joined by top Russian analysts, have made clear that any such new and viable system must include the United States—which means that the United States must abandon its delusions of ruling a unipolar world, which no longer exists, and begin collaborating with major nations for a new and just economic system.

This was highlighted in an Aug. 24 wire of China's official Xinhua news agency, titled "Interview: Russia, China should Cooperate within G-20 to Tackle Challenges." Andrey Kortunov, the Director General of the Russian International Affairs Council, which is close to the Russian Foreign Ministry, said "The longer those reforms are postponed, the higher the risk of new crises and instability in the world economy." He added later, "If today Beijing and Moscow offer their concept of stability to the international community, it is not just empty words, but proposals based on many successful experiences." He noted that the United States can be "a complex, and sometimes unpredictable partner," but nevertheless, "Both Russia and China should consistently seek common ground with Washington, and avoid crises, without making concessions on matters of principle."

A Xinhua commentary on the same day, also regarding the G-20, assailed "over-reliance on monetary policy" and the focus on "markets" as opposed to "nations"—at the expense of policies

> "... To avoid nuclear world war and financial chaos—the results of Obama's failed Presidency—is the leading topic of discussion among world leaders during the international summits over the months of September and October."

aiming for real physical-economic growth, and based on technological innovation. "China will use the conference to spur dialogue among developed and developing countries around the potential to foster growth through reforms and innovation."

The *Wall Street Journal* has suggested that it was at the request of China, that the Bank of International Settlements issued a recent report warning that there are no mechanisms in place at this time which can prevent a blow-out of the $600 trillion-plus global financial derivatives bubble, if any major party defaults. *Business Insider,* in what could be described as a painful understatement, was forced to admit that the results of this survey "are slightly terrifying," because if derivatives clearing-houses fail to handle a crisis, then derivatives become "unexploded nuclear bombs nestling deep in the financial system." The *Wall Street Journal* goes on to note that China has placed the safety of central clearing houses "high on the agenda" of the upcoming G-20 summit.

There is now an increasing and widespread belief among top officials of the trans-Atlantic region, that Europe and the United States are on the very edge of a financial blowout, whose magnitude is equalled only by their own denial both of its global consequences, and of the collapse of western dominance. Bloomberg reported Tuesday, Aug. 23, that Deutsche Bank, Barclays and Credit Suisse are sitting on a combined $102.5 billion in "Level 3" assets,— i.e. assets which are illiquid, without market value, and which cannot be dumped in a crisis. The *Economist* headlined its Aug. 20-26 issue,

"Nightmare on Main Street," warning that the $26 trillion U.S. housing market, which underlies a mountain of derivatives and other bank and non-bank securitized gambling paper,— is again ready to blow.

With the entire political and financial class of the West increasingly discredited, the only remaining option is the immediate reinstatement of Glass-Steagall full bank separation in the United States, and identical implementation throughout Europe. Glass-Steagall, followed by a jubilee debt write-off for the developing nations (in line with Alfred Herrhausen's policy in 1989), and the extension of long-term credit for industrial and scientific development, are just some of the first, indispensable steps towards the creation of a new global financial architecture, and are the prerequisites for a new cultural paradigm, a new Renaissance for all mankind.

The foundations for such a new global financial and economic architecture are now well-established through the growing integration of Eurasia, being woven through cooperation among the Eurasian Economic Union, the Shanghai Cooperation Organization, the BRICS, ASEAN, and other groupings. It is China's "One Belt, One Road" initiative, based on Lyndon and Helga LaRouche's original mid-1990s concept of the Eurasian Landbridge, which is the principle upon which this Eurasian and potentially global development is premised.

As Mexican President Jose Lopez-Portillo once said, "It is now time to listen to the wise words of Lyndon LaRouche!"

EIR Contents

www.larouchepub.com Volume 43, Number 36, September 2, 2016

Cover This Week

The main venue of the 2016 G-20 Summit in Hangzhou, China.

I. The Great Change Under Way

Is Germany Smart Enough To Seize The New Silk Road Opportunity?

by Helga Zepp-LaRouche, chairwoman of the German political party, Civil Rights Movement Solidarity (BüSo)

Aug. 26—While Chancellor Merkel rushes around these days from mini-summit to mini-summit—first on an Italian aircraft carrier, then from one Eastern European capital to the next, in a constant but vain attempt to limit the disintegration process of the European Union—China is entering the last phase of preparation for the G20 summit, which it will chair in Hangzhou. This could be the most promising G20 summit ever, because the Chinese government will put forward a comprehensive concept for how the world economic and financial crisis can be overcome. Whatever the outcome may be, it will become perfectly transparent who is working constructively toward this goal, and who is clinging to the dangerous old geopolitics and failed neoliberal monetary policy.

The European Union (EU) and Washington have every reason to join the successful course of China, and of the Asian states cooperating with China. Since the Brexit, France, Italy, and Austria have gone into competition over who will be the next to leave the EU.

In France, conservative former President Nicolas Sarkozy has launched a new bid for the presidency in a memorandum in which he demands an end to the legal primacy of the EU over French laws, as well as the repeal of the EU's Lisbon Treaty. Socialist candidate Arnaud Monte-bourg pledges to follow General de Gaulle's "empty chair" policy,[1] while the anti-European *Front National* of Marine Le Pen, won 55% in the most recent communal elections and Jacques Cheminade of the *Solidarité et Progrès* party, whose campaign is gaining momentum, is advocating an alliance of sovereign European states. Thus practically all of the relevant presidential

---

1. De Gaulle's "empty chair" policy was his boycott of European Commission institutions in 1965, in protest against policies that threatened national sovereignty with European supranationalism.

Creative Commons/antmoose

The European Central Bank headquarters in Frankfurt, Germany, one of the principal elements of the failed, bankrupt system.

The EU is careening toward dissolution as its members cling to geopolitics and associated bankrupt monetary policy. The "Big 3" of the EU, from left, François Hollande, President of France, Prime Minister of Italy Matteo Renzi, and Chancellor of Germany Angela Merkel in a press conference aboard the Italian helicopter carrier Giuseppe Garibaldi after their Aug. 22, 2016 summit.

candidates are positioning themselves against the EU.

In Italy, Prime Minister Matteo Renzi is quaking at the prospect of the October referendum on the constitution, in whose wake the anti-EU Five Star Movement (M5S) could win new elections held soon afterwards. The next government in Austria will likely be led by the anti-EU Freedom Party of Austria (FPÖ).

Another aspect of the EU's disintegration process was manifest during Merkel's recent visit to the capitals of the Visegrád Group—Hungary, Slovakia, the Czech Republic, and Poland—whose governments vehemently oppose the refugee quotas decreed by the EU and the refugee policy as a whole. Austrian Defense Minister Hans Peter Doskozil called Merkel's policy "irresponsible" and stressed that Austria would not be the "waiting room" for refugees eager to go on to Germany. Hungarian President Orban plans to turn the fence which he had built on Hungary's border into an "insurmount-

French President Charles de Gaulle boycotted EU institutions to protest an attempt by the EU to override the sovereignty of France with a supranationalist policy, which forced the EU policy to be withdrawn.

able wall," which could "stop several hundred thousand people at any given time." Thus, not only is Merkel's "European solution" for the refugee crisis finished, but so also is the Schengen Agreement for movement within Europe without a passport—and with it the basis for the European currency union.

Blame Game of the Clueless

Given all of these diverse centrifugal forces, the stubbornness with which the pro-EU faction clings to the present EU policy seems divorced from reality in the extreme. Instead of addressing the reasons for the growing opposition, it is responding to the Brexit vote with a demand for "more Europe," and is plotting behind closed doors to somehow reverse the Brexit. This has even prompted four of the five economics "Wise Men" (the German Council of Economic Experts) to issue a warning, in a joint article in the *Frankfurter Allgemeine Zeitung* of Aug. 26, that this approach will only strengthen the centrifugal forces.

Unity didn't even prevail at the mini-summit of the "big three"—Merkel, Hollande, and Renzi—pathetically orchestrated on the island of Ventotene in memory of Altiero Spinelli, one of the "fathers of Europe," and held, symbolically, on an Italian aircraft carrier. Hollande and Renzi, with an eye to the economically desolate situation in their countries, pleaded for programs of capital investment; Merkel countered with the usual austerity programs—as if their appeal were not long since passé.

It has even come to the point of

public disagreements between European Central Bank head Mario Draghi (whose dubious role in various bailout operations is currently being investigated) and the European Central Bank, on the one side, and John Michael Cryan and Deutsche Bank (the riskiest bank in the world, according to the IMF), together with CDU parliamentarian Wolfgang Bosbach, Volker Wieland of the Five Wise Men, and Bundesbank Board Member Andreas Dombret on the other. Given this, and the fact that Deutsche Bank is suddenly acting as the advocate for depositors and pensioners in light of the "fatal consequences" of negative interest rates, it should be clear: The blame game has begun. Everyone is blaming everyone else for the collapse of the trans-Atlantic financial system, which everyone knows is fast approaching.

Thus the leading representatives of the EU and the governments of the EU member states have developed the blindness typical of those defending an outmoded model in which they have invested their whole identity. The view of the EU from outside Europe has long since changed. The EU used to be considered a model for regional integration by organizations such as ASEAN or the African Union, as well as by those seeking Latin American integration. But starting with the handling of the Greek crisis by the Troika, and then conclusively with the refugee crisis, that is over and done with. These countries consider the EU a failed model. Only extremely oblivious representatives of the EU or EU governments dare these days to talk about "democracy" and "human rights," in light of Frontex's actions against the refugees and the dubious deals on the refugee question.

For the Good of All Mankind

During the eight years of the Obama Administration, the United States barely got above 1% economic growth per year (by the badly flawed measure of inflation-adjusted GDP). President Franklin D. Roosevelt accomplished as much growth in every one of his first three years in office as Obama has achieved in eight years. And economic growth in the the European Union has been even less than that of the United States in the same timeframe. Meanwhile, China's economic growth went from 9.2% in 2009 to "only" 6.9% in 2015. And in contrast to the casino economy of the trans-Atlantic

censoo.com

The 200th freight-train from Zhengzhou to Hamburg departed February 2016, the cargo rail service between the two cities having begun in July 2013. Chinese President Xi Jinping has asked all European countries to join in the mutual development of the New Silk Road.

sector, the real economy in China is by far the largest economic sector, while the speculative domain is virtually negligible.

During the G20 summit on September 4th and 5th in Hangzhou, China will present a carefully worked out concept as to how to create a stable financial architecture, and how the G20 can be transformed from a mechanism for crisis management into a durable alliance of countries that work together for the common good of the entire world. China's intention is to replace a system based on short term profits with a sound economy which relies on innovation for economic growth.

In the three years since he proposed the development of the New Silk Road internationally, Chinese President Xi Jinping has launched an exemplary success story, in which more than one hundred nations and international organizations are already cooperating. President Xi has repeatedly asked all of the European countries and the United States, especially, to collaborate in the win-win perspective of building the New Silk Road together. The fact that China has invited a large contingent of developing countries to participate in the G20 summit, is a further indication of its serious intent to create a new economic and financial architecture for the entire world.

We Can Learn, Can't We?

In Hangzhou, what Friedrich Schiller once called the "great destiny of mankind" will be on the agenda, namely the question of whether the human family can recognize, in time, that we are all in the same boat, and can only survive if narrow nationalistic and geopolitical interests are supplanted by the common aims of mankind.

A major problem preventing Germany from constructive cooperation with China's future-oriented perspective of developing a new model of cooperation among nations, is the current German tendency to base everything on the "green economy," which seeks to find solutions exclusively "within the ecological limits of planet Earth"—in line with the mantra of the environmentalist movement.

But it is precisely in this area that China is far ahead of the narrow-minded thinking of a two-dimensional world—seeing the world not as flat, but as an aquarium. China has the most ambitious space travel program in the world which, with the coming Chang'e missions, will not only explore the far side of the Moon, but pursue concrete plans to mine large quantities of helium-3 as a raw material for a future fusion economy here on Earth.

The response of the EU and of the United States at this G20 summit will make clear whether they are able to learn. What China, and the Asian nations cooperating with China, represent today is to the benefit of all mankind.

Although the organizations associated or allied with me internationally may be numerically small, we are far superior to our critics in terms of analysis, ideas, and solutions. And it is precisely this capability that we will bring into play to put Europe on the right track.

SEIZE THIS MOMENT!

Historic Vistas Open at Vladivostok and Hangzhou

by David Christie of the LaRouche PAC National Policy Committee

Aug. 31—If you are prepared to think and act for victory, then you will recognize that this is the week that we can begin the final dissolution of the British Empire, forever. Not only that: With it will go the whole, hoary system of empire, which is older than written history, the system rightly called the adolescence of mankind. China's President Xi Jinping is taking personal responsibility for key aspects of the upcoming G-20 Summit in Hangzhou, China, Sept. 4-5, at which the leadership of China intends to sound the death-knell of the financial oligarchy with a new financial architecture. This new architecture is coherent with the physical-economic policy already under way in China, Russia, India, and a growing roster of other key nations which are collaborating on China's "New Silk Road," which is quickly becoming the "World Landbridge" as outlined by Lyndon and Helga LaRouche for more than three decades.

The G-20 Summit in Hangzhou will be immediately preceded by the Eastern Economic Forum in Vladivostok, Russia, Sept. 2-3, where President Vladimir Putin of Russia will be joined by Xi Jinping of China, President Park Geun-Hye of South Korea, and Prime Minister Shinzo Abe of Japan, along with other heads of state from around the world.

Northeast Asia—where Russia, China, Japan, and the Korean Peninsula intersect—represents one of the greatest sources of economic potential in the world. And for that reason, it has been subjected to the British policy of "divide and rule" since the 19th Century. Cooperation among these nations immediately forces the issue of the inevitable Bering Strait tunnel connecting Russia to the Americas. And along with the Bering Strait tunnel, opening up the development of the Arctic should actually be seen as an integral part of an international space program, from the standpoint of both the scientific advances required to develop this vast, inhospitable area and the insights to be gained there into planet Earth's relationship to its Solar-system and Galactic environment.

At the Vladivostok Eastern Economic Forum, Dmitry Rogozin, chairman of Russian space agency Roscosmos, will address a panel on "The Space Agenda

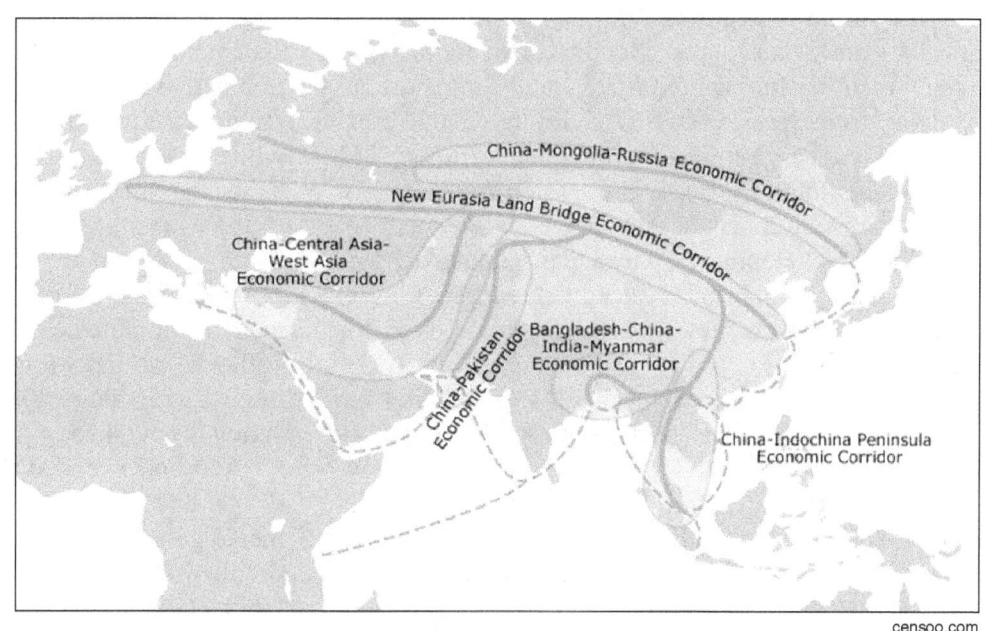

censoo.com

The rapidly emerging transportation and development corridors, which are the basis for the collaboration of all nations in a new worldwide paradigm.

Russian President Vladimir Putin (left), and President of China Xi Jinping at the November 2014 APEC Economic Leaders' Meetings.

kremlin.ru

for the Asia-Pacific," along with space officials from Asian nations. While there is no panel on exploration or development of the Arctic *per se*, there is one on the integrally related Northern Sea Route. There are many more panels to discuss infrastructure and energy projects, opportunities for investors, and vehicles and instruments for supporting entrepreners.

The forum is expected to draw upwards of 2,400 guests from China, Japan, South Korea, India, Vietnam, Australia, the United States, and Singapore, as well as from Russia itself. According to the press office of Russia's Far East Development Ministry, 161 agreements totalling nearly 1.6 trillion rubles ($24.5 billion) are expected to be signed. Russia's Minister of Far East Development, Alexander Galushka, told TASS that a number of these agreements will be related to creation of new production facilities in the region.

A Russia-Japan panel will have 15 speakers from the top leadership of business in both countries, including the chairmen of Mitsui, Fujitsu, and Sofbank corporations, and the Governor of Hokkaido. A Russia-South Korea panel will include the presidents of Hyundai Engineering and Construction, and of Samsung Electronics. According to Yonhap News Agency, South Korea and Russia "also agreed to seek a free trade agreement between South Korea and the Russia-led Eurasian Economic Union (EAEU), which has Kazakhstan, Belarus, Armenia, and Kyrgyzstan as members." Russia and South Korea are also discussing railway development. At Vladivostok, there will also be a panel for Russia and the Association of Southeast Asian Nations (ASEAN) with high-level representation. There will also be a Russia-Germany panel, but the only German there will be the chairman of the Russian-German Chamber of Commerce, because German Chancellor Angela Merkel has succumbed to Barack Obama's anti-Russian agenda.

Were Japan and South Korea to consolidate their shift towards the expanding conception of China's New Silk Road and fully integrate themselves into this new Eurasian perspective, the implications would be tectonic. The forces of the British Empire have embroiled this region in geopolitical manipulations for more than a century, and now, through their control of the U.S. Presidency of Barack Obama, they are putting heavy pressure on Japan and South Korea to keep them obedient.

Nevertheless, there have been breaks in this situation. UN Secretary General Ban Ki-moon, who is also an important political figure in South Korea, has made statements in support of China's initiatives in connection with the G-20 Summit in Hangzhou. Ban may be a factor in the upcoming presidential elections there. And while China has taken the initiative to put the new financial architecture on the agenda at the G-20, in light of the worsening financial breakdown of the trans-Atlantic system of the City of London and Wall Street, Prime Minister Shinzo Abe of Japan, on his part, has made clear statements on the danger of the unfolding collapse, and has warned that the world economy faces the risk of another 2008 "Lehman shock" if appropriate action is not taken.

Abe had intended that a mention of this financial danger be inserted into the final communiqué of the G-7 meeting earlier this year. He has said that the present problems cannot be solved by monetary policy alone. Unlike Obama and his British masters, Prime Minister Abe understands that physical economic growth is required.

kremlin.ru

Russia President Putin (center right), hosting Japanese Prime Minister Shinzo Abe and high-level members of their respective staffs, in Sochi, Russia, on March 6, 2016.

Tectonic Shifts

Never forget that the world is undergoing a massive strategic recalibration. People and institutions which may not have been on the side of humanity—which may not have encouraged its development, or even actively engaged in genocidal actions against their fellows—*can change*, even if not always for the most noble reasons.

Take for example a recent article by Gal Luft in *Foreign Affairs*, the journal of the U.S. Council on Foreign Relations. In "China's Infrastructure Play: Why Washington Should Accept the New Silk Road," Luft extols the virtues of China's Silk Road program. Or take the case of the Chairman of the Munich Security Conference, Wolfgang Ischinger, who now says "the Turkish about-face on Assad is comprehensible," and urges the West to "find it comprehensible." Ischinger notes, furthermore, that those who demanded that Assad leave office as a starting point, had "a failed plan."

A Damascus Road conversion? *Realpolitik*? Or just plain opportunism? Whatever the reason, or however long it lasts in an individual case, it shows that something is in the air. With this potential for change, it is now incumbent upon those of us in the trans-Atlantic area who understand the absolute necessity for urgent change, to move for victory.

It is in this context that the strategic implications of Japan's and South Korea's shifting towards the New Paradigm are so immense. President Park of South Korea went to China in 2015 for the 70th anniversary celebration of the end of World War II in the Pacific. She sat next to Putin and Xi in an important and significant gesture. Later, however, she yielded to the excruciating pressure that Barack Obama brought down upon her and consented to the placement of the Terminal High Altitude Aerial Defense (THAAD) system in Korea, which has caused both Russia and China to register grave concerns that the strategic balance is being upset.

But at the same time, in the lead-up to the Vladivostok forum, Russia and Japan are working out the details for a long-delayed peace treaty which will formally end World War II between them. Abe has apparently referred to a "new approach," but it remains to be determined what that approach actually is.

In reality, the war that must be ended in that region goes back much further than World War II—it even goes back further than World War I,— back to the British-instigated wars along geopolitical fault lines on the Korean Peninsula and the adjacent area formerly known as Manchuria, at the intersection of Russia, China, and Korea. These were wars designed to stop the spread of Hamilton's "American System," which had taken root in Japan at the time of the Meiji Restoration in the 1860s.

World War II Goes Back Centuries

Halford Mackinder is generally considered the godfather of British Geopolitics, and was the Director of the London School of Economics and Political Science at the time he wrote his seminal paper, "The Geographical Pivot of History," which was presented to an audience at the Royal Geographical Society in 1904 and published in its journal. The Russo-Japanese War began in the same year (Feb. 8, 1904 to Sept. 5, 1905), that is, about a decade after the first Sino-Japanese War (Aug. 1, 1894 to April 17, 1895). The second Sino-Japanese War (1937-1945) was part of World War II, which then flowed into the Cold War, and has now brought us into the anteroom of the *end of war*, one way or the other— either through the thermonuclear annihilation of civilization or even of mankind,—or else the end of war through the policy of mutual benefit, represented by the New Silk Road of China.

Mackinder and his accomplices were not passive observers of these wars, but were actively organizing the "divide and conquer" strategy on behalf of the British Monarchy and its global enforcement program formerly known as the British East India Company. Following this strategy, they manipulated populations along ethnic and religious lines on the Eurasian landmass; they simultaneously controlled commerce on the seas and the related usurious banking and insurance operations. Mackinder was fairly frank about his mission as he outlined it in "The Geographical Pivot of History," particularly about his concern lest Russia become a bridge between Europe and Asia.

On the opposing, humanist side, the great German philosopher and founder of physical economy, Wilhelm Gottfried Leibniz (1646-1716), had considered that since Russia shared in both Asian and European culture, it was uniquely positioned to act as a bridge between Christian Europe and Confucian China.

As that bridge between Asia and Europe began to take literal, physical form as the Trans-Siberian Railway (built 1891-1916), Mackinder expressed his concern:

> The Russian railways have a clear run of 6,000 miles from Wirballen in the west to Vladivostok in the east. The Russian army in Manchuria is as significant evidence of mobile land-power as the British army in South Africa was of sea-power. True, that the Trans-Siberian railway is still a single and precarious line of communication, but the century will not be old before all Asia is covered with railways. The spaces within the Russian Empire and Mongolia are so vast, and their potentialities in population, wheat, cotton, fuel, and metals so incalculably great, that it is inevitable that a vast economic world, more or less apart, will there develop inaccessible to oceanic commerce.

Halford Mackinder, the godfather of British Empire geopolitics.

The Trans-Siberian Railroad was an echo of Abraham Lincoln's Trans-Continental Railroad. After the Civil War, the United States had emerged as the greatest economic power in the world by employing the principles of Alexander Hamilton—by raising the productive powers of labor through access to infrastructure and employing a credit system in the form of "Greenbacks." Lincoln's economic adviser, Henry C. Carey, had unleashed a global revolution of Hamilton's "American System" against the "British System" of debt slavery—as well as literal slavery. One of Carey's students, Erasmus Peshine Smith, became an adviser to Japan's Emperor Meiji, while another, Friedrich List of Germany, proposed "The Railway Line from Ostende [Belgium] to Bombay." Sergei Witte, the Russian Tsar's Finance Minister who greatly accelerated the construction of the Trans-Siberian Railroad, based his own policies on those of List.

Mackinder knew that Germany, in collaboration with a Russia acting as a bridge between Europe and Asia, would be the end of the British Empire. This mantra from Mackinder's 1919 book, *Democratic Ideals and Reality*, expresses his geopolitical outlook:

First Viscount Alfred Milner. Lord Milner played a leading role in implementing the domination of the world by the British Empire.

> Who rules East Europe commands the Heartland [the territory of Russia at that time].
>
> Who rules the Heartland commands the World-Island [Eurasia and Africa].
>
> Who rules the World-Island commands the world.

The subversive British Imperial operations were extensive in their attempt to prevent development by fostering chaos in the eastern part of Europe—such as the Balkans, which was the center of Friedrich List's proposal for the Berlin to Baghdad rail line. However, the British fear that the extensive railroad development plan of Chinese independence leader Sun Yat-sen might merge with the Trans-Siberian Railroad was just as intense as their fear of development in the eastern part of Europe. So they set their sights on blowing up the Korean Peninsula and the adjacent area then known as Manchuria. Charles Addis of the Hong Kong and Shanghai Bank and Thomas Lamont of J.P. Morgan created a consortium that prevented loans from being made for the development plans of Sun Yat-sen, while at the same time Lamont organized U.S. financial support for Japan's invasion of Manchuria.

Leopold Amery was a protégé of Lord Milner.

Thus Manchuria and the Korean peninsula were embroiled in the Russo-Japanese War and the Sino-Japanese Wars, rather than becoming a nexus-point for Sun Yat-sen's extensive railroad grid linking Asia to Europe through the Trans-Siberian Railroad. That would have used the economic potential of Japan under the Meiji Restoration to develop all of the nations surrounding the Korean Peninsula. Instead, Japan was brought into Mackinder's vision of the encirclement of Eurasia, to prevent nations from collaborating through development corridors.

"Britain, Canada, the United States, South Africa, Australia, and Japan are now a ring of outer and insular bases of sea-power and commerce, inaccessible to the land-power of Euro-Asia," Mackinder wrote.

But Is It True?

Mackinder's geopolitical theory would continue to be implemented through one of his followers, Karl Haushofer, the geopolitical theorist for the Nazis. The Nazis continued to unfold that British Empire-directed Hell, which essentially continues down to today, with the same targets and the same underlying misconception of the nature of humanity. But do any of his followers actually believe Mackinder's theory? Did Mac-

kinder even believe his own theory? Some of the quotes from the "Geographical Pivot of History" give an insight into the method of the British Empire, but they do not necessarily indicate Mackinder's sense of causality. As the name implies, Mackinder's "geopolitics" incorporates the belief that geography and the condition of the land have the determining role in shaping the political economy of a society.

But is that how history is shaped? Was the history of Europe, and its civilization and culture, defined by the invasions of the Mongol hordes, or by the marauding Vikings, as Mackinder implies here?

For a thousand years a series of horse-riding peoples emerged from Asia through the broad interval between the Ural Mountains and the Caspian Sea, rode through the open spaces of southern Russia, and struck home into Hungary in the very heart of the European peninsula, shaping by the necessity of opposing them the history of each of the great peoples around—the Russians, the Germans, the French, the Italians, and the Byzantine Greeks. That they stimulated healthy and powerful reaction, instead of crushing opposition under a widespread despotism, was due to the fact that the mobility of their power was conditioned by the steppes, and necessarily ceased in the surrounding forests and mountains.

A rival mobility of power was that of the Vikings in their boats. Descending from Scandinavia both upon the northern and the southern shores of Europe, they penetrated inland by the river ways. But the scope of their action was limited, for, broadly speaking, their power was effective only in the neighborhood of the water.

Mackinder even tries to suggest that it was the pressure of these invading hordes from the Steppes of Russia and Mongolia by land, and by the Vikings from the sea, that created the great bond between France and England. What bunk!

In truth, it doesn't matter whether Mackinder actu-

One of the projects for which financing will be sought at the Sept. 2-3 Eastern Economic Forum is the construction of a transport corridor that will link Khabarovsk, on the Trans-Siberian Railroad, more directly to the Pacific Ocean. The port (above) will be expanded to a universal sea port.

as a power to defeat all others. Unfortunately, the policy-makers of the British Empire did not conclude from this that it would be in their interest to promote creativity among all of their subjects. Instead, the Empire has always sought to beat that creativity out of everyone on the planet, to make the hegemony of its own leadership unassailable.

The Empire's approach is not working very well, and a never-ending series of potential upshifts for humanity is now on the horizon. Nowhere is that potential more alive than in the far east of Eurasia. The principal nations represented at the Eastern Economic Forum in Vladivostok this weekend—China, Russia, Japan, and Korea—represent some of the greatest scientific power on the planet. The Vladivostok meeting is nominally about the development of the Far East, which immediately puts the Bering Strait tunnel implicitly on the agenda. The mineral and energy wealth of Siberia could never be accessed without development corridors, and the same is true for Alaska and northern Canada—and therefore a commitment to that development opens the door for the Bering Strait connection.

However, the development of the Arctic regions of Siberia and North America can only be accomplished if it is seen as subset of an international space program. The conditions there are extremely harsh, even brutal. There is therefore a need to explore options for providing semi-artificial conditions akin to living in space or on other planets. Moreover, the psychological implications of living in semi-artificial environments and the effects of the fluctuations in light exposure in the far North can be studied to gain insights useful for longer term space exploration. And, while we know that the Aurora Borealis is extremely beautiful, we have more to learn about its reason for existence. We assume it speaks to us of the relations of our Earth with the Solar system, the Galaxy, and our Universe beyond.

ally believed this or not. What it represents is something that is a common affliction for many people—the obsessive belief that there is some external factor that shapes the development of humanity other than human creativity. Mackinder's theory that geography defines the development of humanity is not really unlike the dogma of those who think that an economy is, or should be, shaped by an alleged "free market."

The Failure of Empire

After Mackinder read his paper to the Geographical Society, Leo Amery responded in an interesting way. Amery was a protégé of Lord Alfred Milner, and both would play a crucial role in shaping the policy of the British Empire over the next decades. Amery clearly didn't buy Mackinder's "Heartland" argument. Instead, he revealed what any empire must crush—the mind.

> The successful powers will be those who have the greatest industrial basis. It will not matter whether they are in the center of a continent or on an island; those people who have the industrial power and the power of invention and of science will be able to defeat all others.

Amery views the world from the vantage point of an imperial foot-soldier: Rather than seeing the power of science and invention to advance all humanity, he sees it

Every Day Counts In Today's Showdown To Save Civilization

That's why you need EIR's **Daily Alert Service**, a strategic overview compiled with the input of Lyndon LaRouche, and delivered to your email 5 days a week.

For example: On Jan. 7, EIR's Daily Alert featured the British hand behind the pattern of global provocations toward war. Of special note is British Intelligence's role in instigating the Saudi Kingdom's attempt to set off a Sunni-Shia war. This religious war has been the intent of British strategy since the Blair-Bush attack on Iraq in 2003.

We also uniquely update you regularly on the progress toward the release of the suppressed 28 pages of the Congressional Inquiry on 9/11, which would expose the Saudi role.

Every edition highlights the reality of the impending financial crash/bail-in policies that would realize the British goal of mass depopulation.

This is intelligence you need to act on, if we are going to survive as a nation and a species. Can you really afford to be without it?

THURSDAY, JANUARY 7, 2016

Volume 2, Number 97

EIR Daily Alert Service

P.O. Box 17390, Washington, DC 20041-0390

- British Crown Pushing War and Genocide in 2016
- Financial Mudslide Goes On; Monetarist Tyranny Gloats over Bail-Ins
- Moody's Downgrades Portugal's Novo Banco
- Puerto Rico's Default: It's Every Vulture for Himself
- Wide Glass-Steagall Debate Set Off Again by Sanders Speech
- MI6 Mouthpiece Evans-Pritchard Touts Persian Gulf Chaos
- North Korea Tests a Miniaturized Hydrogen Bomb
- Uighur Terrorists Found in Indonesia
- Foreign Investors Are Flocking In to China

EDITORIAL

British Crown Pushing War and Genocide in 2016

II. The New Scientific Revolution

Destination Moon? The Next Frontier For the Common Aims of All Mankind

by Kesha Rogers and Ben Deniston

"The Moon is the touchstone of the human future."

—Krafft Ehricke

Aug. 28—China is opening up a new frontier in mankind's exploration of the Galaxy! Earlier this year, China announced that it plans to be the first nation to land on the far side of the Moon, when it launches its Chang'e 4 mission in 2018. This comes in the context of increasing interest, on the part of China and Russia, in returning mankind to the Moon, possibly including permanently manned bases. China is taking global leadership in mankind's conquest of space.

Lyndon LaRouche responded to these developments by calling for a full mapping of the Moon, especially the far side. While the lunar far side has been imaged and investigated from lunar orbit, mankind is far from uncovering all of the secrets the lunar far side is hiding, and can only imagine what the implications of tomorrow's discoveries will be for transforming mankind's relation to the Solar system and beyond.

China's lunar exploration program clearly indicates that China is not just making a new landing site on the Moon's surface, but opening up to mankind what German-American space pioneer and aeronautical engineer Krafft Ehricke once described as the "seventh continent" of the world. By doing so, China—in collaboration with Russia and other nations—establishes mankind as a truly polyglobal species.

Ehricke and the Common Aims of Mankind

The world is moving forward, and the vision for a new paradigm is already in being, despite the refusal of the United States to join in the win-win cooperation offered by China for the benefit and progress of all nations.

Instead, President Barack Obama has dismantled and privatized our U.S. manned space program, bailed out the bankrupt speculators of Wall Street as they continue to plunder the physical economy, and launched a series of illegal wars around the world. By aborting the Constellation program—which focussed on the Moon

White House Photo/Pete Souza

Former astronaut and Senator, John Glenn, expressed his concern over the idling of the U.S. manned space program in this July 19, 2010 meeting with President Obama. Obama had announced his radical change in the direction of NASA on April 15, 2010. Left to right: Dr. John Holdren, director of the Office of Science and Technology; Glenn; Obama; Rob Nabors, senior adviser to the chief of staff.

President John Kennedy is inspecting the interior of Friendship 7, the capsule in which John Glenn (to the right of Kennedy) became the first American to orbit Earth.

as a critical, permanent destination for the exploration and development of space—Obama eliminated our nation's ability to lead a manned presence in space for the foreseeable future. Not only has the project to return to and develop the Moon been scrapped under Obama, but an insane project to capture an asteroid was set up to replace it. Meanwhile, research on thermonuclear fusion power has also been cut.

How long will Americans condone such insanity? We must demand a restoration of a national mission for the development of space outlined by such visionary leaders as President Kennedy and Krafft Ehricke, who saw the Moon not just as a temporary attraction or landing ground, but essential to mankind's development of the Solar system.

China's emphasis on lunar development, with its focus on landing on the lunar far side, is a critical phase of a science-driver program essential to international cooperation and economic development around the planet and beyond. Lunar exploration and space development must be defined in terms of a program for economic development of the Moon, needed in conjunction with a crash program for fusion power, as described by Lyndon LaRouche as a shared vision of his and his wife Helga's association and friendship with Krafft Ehricke.

Ehricke also envisioned and mapped such a program in great detail. In his 1985 article on "Lunar Industrialization and Settlement," he states, "The most important aspect of lunar development lies in the human sector. It bears repeating that technological progress and environmental expansion are no substitutes for human growth and maturity, but they can help the human reach higher maturity and wisdom." He explains,

Human growth is contingent not only on the absence of war, or overcoming hunger, poverty, and social injustice—but the presence of overarching, elevating goals, and their associated perspectives. Expanding into space needs to be understood and approached as world development, as a positive, peaceful, growth-oriented, macrosociological project, whose goal is to ultimately release humanity from its present parasitic, embryonic bondage in the biospheric womb of one planet. This will demand immense human creativity, courage, and maturity."

It is with these common aims of mankind in mind that nations around the world, led by China and Russia, in defining a unified *mission* for the unfolding of mankind's truly creative nature, take up the Moon as a stepping stone destination for mankind's development of space. China's statement of principle for space exploration declares that, "Outer space is the commonwealth of mankind. Exploration, development, and utilization of outer space are an unremitting pursuit of mankind."

China and Russia Take the Lead

China's lunar exploration program is currently leading the way. In December 2013 the world was gripped with excitement when China made the first soft landing on the Moon in 40 years with its Chang'e 3 mission carrying the Yutu rover. Now China has announced that its 2018 Chang'e 4 mission will make mankind's first ever landing on the far side of the Moon.

Because the Moon makes one rotation on its axis in the same time that it takes to complete one orbital rotation around the Earth, the same side of the Moon is always facing our home planet, leaving the far side shrouded in mystery.

Although the far side was imaged from lunar orbit in 1959 by the Soviet Union—and at higher resolution in 1967-1968 by NASA's Lunar Reconnaissance

Fusion/Christopher Sloan

An artist's depiction of Selenopolis, Krafft Ehricke's city on the Moon, housing thousands and powered by fusion reactors, seen under construction on the right. The city is connected to mining and manufacturing sites on other parts of the Moon. The industrial development of the Moon will process lunar materials, including those obtained by underground mining.

Chang'e 4 will also continue China's investigation into critical questions of the distribution of water, metals, and other potential resources, including the superb fusion fuel helium-3, which is almost absent on the Earth. Approximately 50 tons of it could power the entire United States for one year. It is thought that the far side, and possibly the Aitken basin specifically, could have higher concentrations of helium-3. Top Chinese officials have made clear their interest in developing the Moon's helium-3 resources to power the Earth for thousands of years into the future.

The lunar far side can also open up a completely new window for viewing the universe. The Earth is a very noisy place, especially in certain lower frequencies of radio waves, making it impossible to observe the low-frequency radio sky from Earth or Earth orbit. This is the last major, unexplored region of the electromagnetic spectrum in terms of imaging the universe, and it can

Orbiter—mankind has barely scratched the surface. In discussions over the past week, Lyndon LaRouche called for a full mapping and investigation of the lunar far side, and everything it may represent for mankind.

For example, the geology on the far side—as we know it so far from photography and radar (microwave) imaging—is anomalous compared to the near side. It provides a relatively undisturbed record of the early history of the Moon, but it also preserves traces that can tell us about the changing and developing Solar system and the Galaxy beyond. The Chinese have wisely chosen to land the Chang'e 4 mission in a particularly interesting location on the far side, the Aitken basin near the south pole. It is possibly the largest, deepest, and oldest impact crater on the Moon.

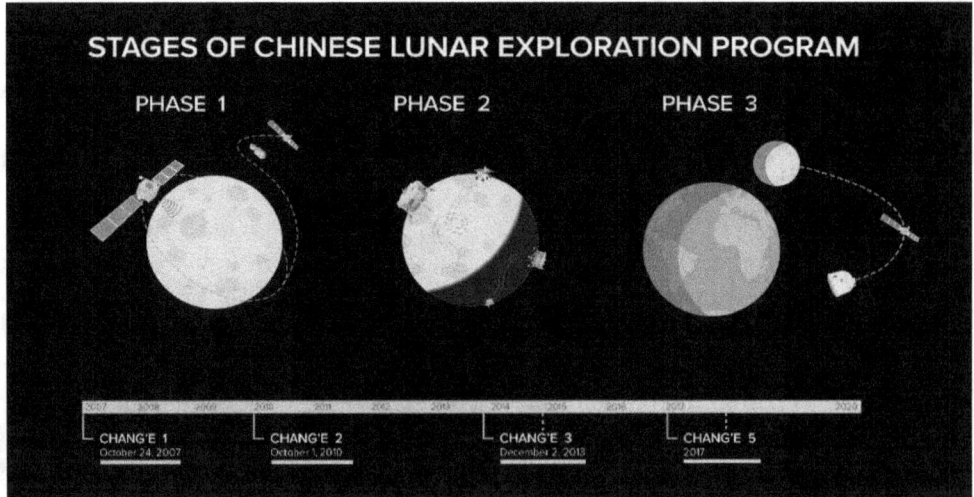

China launched its Lunar Exploration Program in 2004, to be carried out in three phases: 1. to orbit the Moon and capture lunar surface images; 2. to achieve unmanned landing on the surface of the Moon and deploy a lunar rover to explore the landing area; 3. to return lunar samples to the Earth.

uniquely be opened up from the lunar far side, where observation systems would be shielded from the Earth's radio noise. Again, China is making the first steps towards exploiting this window by including low-frequency radio observation systems on the 2018 Chang'e 4 far side landing mission.

China's lunar exploration program—which also includes sample returns as part of the Chang'e 5 and Chang'e 6 missions—is laying the groundwork for the fulfillment of Ehricke's vision for the permanent development of the Moon.

Russia, long having declared its interest in a permanent lunar base, is accelerating its efforts to develop a new "super heavy-lift rocket," capable of bringing manned missions to the Moon, something which hasn't existed since Apollo's Saturn V rocket. Russia's first systems could be ready as soon as the early 2020s, and China is looking at the early 2030s for the readiness of its own super heavy-lift rocket system.

Chinese scientists are also working on a feasibility study for a manned radar station on the near side of the Moon, capable of generating high-intensity beams that can reach the Earth and be reflected back to the lunar station, to provide unique data on Earth's extreme weather conditions, global earthquake activity, the polar ice caps, and more.

Other plans for manned lunar development are either in the works or being discussed, including by the head of the European Space Agency. At last, under the leading efforts of China and Russia, the beginnings of Ehricke's vision appear to be on the horizon.

Krafft Ehricke declared, "Our work in space will change Earth's present closed world environment into an open one with access to vast space resources and other critically needed benefits that will greatly improve the lives of all people, and preserve Earth at its best—as man's home and garden for the maximum human future."

These goals, defining a common mission for the progress of all mankind, cannot be accomplished in a paradigm defined by the thermonuclear war threat, the ongoing economic collapse, and the bestialization of human beings, keeping them in an embryonic stage of immaturity. Only through the forming of a new paradigm and the opening of the age of reason will we come to fully realize our truly human potential.

The Lessons of the Italian Earthquake

by Claudio Celani

Aug. 28—I woke up at 4:30 AM Aug. 24 and turned on the Italian television news. I have lived in Germany for many years, but my cable television provider offers some Italian channels.

The announcer was reporting on a severe earthquake in central Italy, but it was not clear where. A news ticker ran along the bottom of the screen, and suddenly I noticed: "Arquata del Tronto." That is in the province of Ascoli Piceno, my birthplace and where my relatives and friends live.

I dialed my brother-in-law's cellphone and he answered. He and my sister had been knocked off their bed by the strong shock and immediately left the house where they live, in the countryside, to reach my mother's townhouse, which is more solid. Their house might be damaged,— how severely will be clear with the daylight. I spoke to all three of them. A lot of fear, but thank God nothing more.

I reached other friends. One was out in the street, like most of the inhabitants of Ascoli. Another was at home; the rest of his family, though, had left the apartment and joined the crowd on the streets. A trained physicist, he was confident that the aftershocks would follow the statistical model and be of lower intensity, and saw no reason to leave the building. A third friend, a doctor at the hospital, said her family was unhurt, but her aged parents were so afraid that they were moving to a safer place on the Adriatic coast.

It was a strong, long, and frightening shock. There were reports of victims, but it was too early to say how many. A few minutes after the shock, rescue teams were on the way, directed to the mountain areas close to the epicenter. Contrary to some international media reports, the rescue machine was highly efficient. Many persons were pulled alive from under the rubble, and the injured were flown to hospitals in Ascoli, Rieti, and L'Aquila. Food, medication, and tents were available immediately, as well as specialized personnel.

As the day progressed, and aftershocks occurred, the full dimensions of the tragedy unfolded. Villages such as Pescara del Tronto and Accumoli were levelled. Tens of victims were reported there and in the larger village of Arquata. These are places I have been intimately familiar with since my childhood. My

RT video grab

Rescue teams, shown in an Aug. 24 live broadcast by RT, looking for survivors after a quake of 6.2 on the Mercalli scale struck Amatrice, Italy.

mother's family comes from Montegallo, a village next to Arquata, and my grandparents are buried there. My mother herself was in Montegallo until two days earlier, benefiting from the fresh air there in the hot month of August. Later on, I learned that the hotel where she stayed was so damaged that it was condemned.

Besides frequent family excursions to the area, as a boy I had spent two weeks of every year in a summer camp there. At the end of our stay, we would climb Monte Vettore, the highest in the Sibillini chain, elevation 2,478 meters or 8,123 feet.

Arquata, which had the highest toll of human lives lost in Ascoli Piceno Province (an Italian province is comparable to a U.S. county) with 46 dead, is on state road 4, which follows pretty much the route of the old Salaria (the salt road) that connected Rome to Ascoli, and beyond that to the Adriatic Sea. Further west in the direction of Rome, closer to the epicenter and already in the province of Rieti, one comes to Accumoli and Amatrice. The latter is known for having invented the famous culinary specialty "spaghetti all'Amatriciana." Amatrice is also rich in Renaissance and pre-Renaissance monuments, and is the birthplace of Cola d'Amatrice, a famous architect who was a collaborator of Raphael.

In this area, four regions are adjoined: Marche, Umbria, Abruzzi, and Latium. The local population lives on agriculture and tourism: the survivors have lost not only their homes, but also their jobs.

Today, Amatrice is half-destroyed. Two hundred twenty-five people died, killed by the collapse of houses that in many cases were four centuries old. Those houses were built after the town had been destroyed in a similar earthquake in the 17th Century. They were built of stone, some surmounted by a cement roof. But newer houses, which had been or should have been built with anti-seismic techniques, also collapsed. Such is the case of a school which is now the object of a criminal investigation.

What Must Be Learned

The final reckoning of the earthquake is 291 dead and 2,500 homeless. This is simultaneously a tragedy and an indictment of the budget policies implemented by the European Union.

If the necessary investments had been made, there would not have been one victim to mourn today. Italy is a seismic area—the peninsula is crossed from north to south by the fault between the African tectonic plate and the Eurasian plate. Over the last 2,500 years, there have been over 30 thousand quakes of magnitude higher than 4 and 5 on the Mercalli linear scale of 1 to 12, and about 560 quakes higher than grade 8. The latter were thirty times as strong as the quake that just hit Amatrice and Arquata.

Thus, nothing justifies the fact that in the towns close to the epicenter, so many houses collapsed and people died. Even if many of them were centuries old and were built of stone, such buildings should have been made safe with known modern building techniques. That this is possible, was shown by the town of Norcia, as close to the epicenter as the destroyed towns, where not one house collapsed and no one died. As the mayor of Norcia explained to the media, this is the result of a serious prevention program implemented in the last decade by the regional authorities, after an earthquake of similar magnitude struck in 1997, with its epicenter in Foligno.

A national prevention program has been on the agenda for decades, dating back to the discovery of such modern techniques, but despite promises by government after government, nothing has been done. The reason is the balanced budget policy which has been imposed on Italy by the Euro system, most strictly since 1992, which become more deadly after 2011. The result is that in the last forty years, it has been calculated that 150 billion euros have been spent in reconstruction after earthquakes, and, astonishingly, merely one billion have been spent for prevention. Professor Armando Zambrano, chairman of the National Council of Engineers, said that a comprehensive national plan to make old houses and buildings safe, might cost up to 100 billion euros. But even if it costs more, it will be money well spent and will save lives.

Budget cuts have also included an awful reduction in university programs in Geology, a key department for mapping seismic activity. From a total of 29 in 2010, there are now only 8, as a result of a 2010 reform that shut down all departments with fewer than 40 teachers.

Additionally, research on earthquake precursors, which is very important, is completely unsupported by the government. Yet the study of precursors is very promising, as shown by researcher Giampaolo Giuliani, who predicted the 2009 L'Aquila earthquake by monitoring radon gas emissions, and warned again

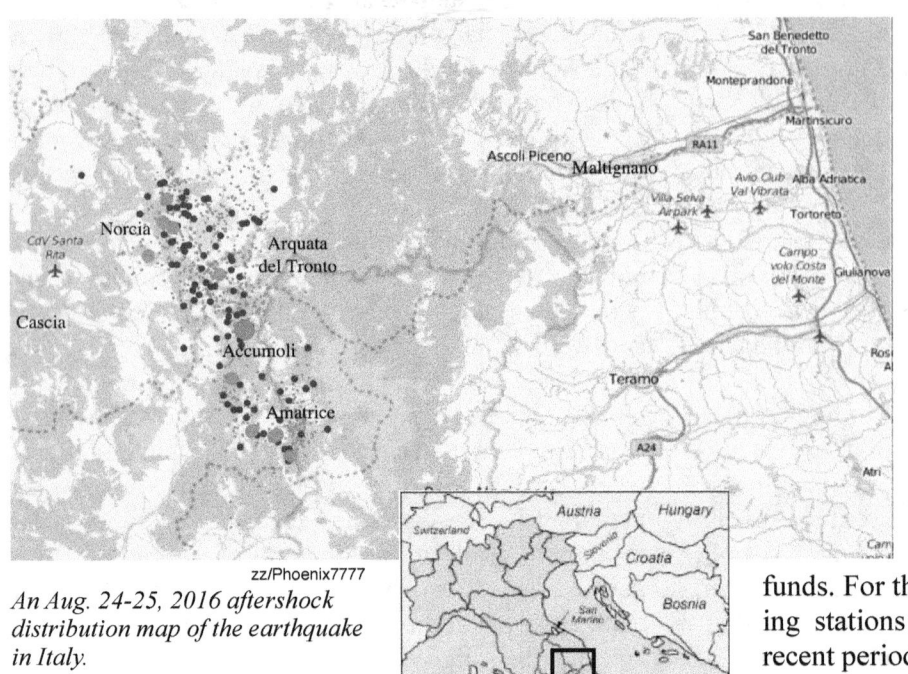

An Aug. 24-25, 2016 aftershock distribution map of the earthquake in Italy.

of a coming seismic event by monitoring an increased level of radon. On his Facebook page, Giuliani on Aug. 10 had published a chart of the seismic anomalies, which were part of the earthquake swarm that led to the earthquake on Aug. 24. "At that time I was in California, and while monitoring stations in Italy, I grasped the presence of an anomaly that in the following days gave birth to four earthquakes in the area," Giuliani said in an interview with *affaritaliani.it*

On Aug. 6, Giuliani had also warned of a "slight increase in radon flux observed in the last hour from one of the stations in Abruzzo."

However, one parameter is insufficient to make exact forecasts. In fact, in 2009 Giuliani had forecast the epicenter to be in Sulmona, and had authorities acted on that forecast, they would have evacuated the population, or part of it, to L'Aquila, thereby creating more victims.

Nevertheless, radon is one parameter to be included in a multi-parameter system including satellites, that, if adequately developed, could one day allow us to forecast, if not all, at least certain earthquakes.

But this research receives no government money. Scientists such as Professor Pier Francesco Biagi, of

Bari University, have built detector systems which have been collecting precious data in the framework of the International Network of Frontier Research on Earthquakes (INFREP), a group which includes scientists from many nations. However, they are obliged to organize private funds to finance their research, funds which are not always there. Indeed, Professor Biagi reported to *EIR* that he had had a detector only 30 km distant from the epicenter of the latest earthquake, but was forced to unplug it and send it to Romania, because of a lack of funds. For the same reason, Biagi's three remaining stations in Italy have been inactive in the recent period.

On Aug. 20, 2009, after the L'Aquila earthquake, Professor Biagi issued a note calling for a national government institution to study earthquake precursors. Biagi started with two considerations: "The first is that those scientists who publish seismic forecasts, at any level, are wrong; the second is that those scientists who insist that earthquake forecasting is impossible are also wrong. Results obtained in the last twenty years have revealed that forecasting an earthquake is not possible in the absolute. At the point when research in this field will have developed better defined techniques and increased the degree of their reliability, some forecasts can be made successfully, even if not everywhere and not every time. In any case, a national institution should be created to this purpose." That call was ignored.

Italian Prime Minister Matteo Renzi has now promised that the time has come for a change, and his cabinet ministers are calling for separating the costs of damage "prevention" from deficit accounting to avoid violating European Union budget rules.

However, Italy should ask no one for permission to do that. A national program must be drafted and implemented under Italian law, regardless of what so-called "EU law" says. Unfortunately, although Renzi plays the great leader and stages European summits on an aircraft carrier, the man giving the orders sits in the European Central Bank bunker in Frankfurt, and the line from there is: let them eat cake.

www.ingramcontent.com/pod-product-compliance
Lightning Source LLC
Chambersburg PA
CBHW051953280526
45789CB00009B/3277